TABLE OF CONTENTS

I0414248

PREFACE

The idea for this Strategy Research Project developed gradually during the first three months at the U.S. Army War College, Class of 2004. Iraq was in turmoil. While "decisive operations" had triumphed in seemingly record time, post-conflict/reconstruction operations appeared "bogged down" in a kaleidoscope of violence ranging from looting, suicide bombers, and outright insurgency. Editorials became fond of using Vietnam comparisons. Initially, I became interested in delving into the complexities of "winning" the peace.

Preliminary research into Phase IV operations in Iraq revealed that the myriad of studies, pre- and post-war, had apparently overlooked the British experience in Mesopotamia during the First World War. I found this omission especially puzzling, since both campaigns took place on literally the very same ground. Even the increasingly a-historical mindset of the twenty-first century should have seen some "utility" in examining this earlier experience.

A comparative analysis of two case studies does not lend itself well to the limits of a Strategy Research Project (SRP). The wealth of material available on both campaigns taxed my writing abilities given the constraints on length. The completed product runs the risk of appearing superficial as a result. Nonetheless, I decided that the comparative analysis warranted completion, no matter how limited. It highlights certain, remarkable similarities between the two campaigns. Indeed, it frankly makes the failure to look at the British Mesopotamian Campaign that much more amazing.

I owe particular thanks to my advisor, Dr. Conrad Crane, Director of the U.S. Army Military History Institute (MHI). He assumed this role despite a host of other special projects and tasks. His meticulous dissection of my drafts was a priceless instrument of quality control. This SRP is a far superior product because of his dedication.

I extend the warmest gratitude to the monumentally-selfless, always-cheerful staff of the Military History Institute. They never flagged in their enthusiasm to assist my research in any way imaginable. They educated me as to just how great a national treasure the MHI is.

I encourage future researchers to delve more deeply. I thus attempted a comprehensive Selected Bibliography. More specifically, I recommend that they track down Gertrude Bell's Review of the Civil Administration. Time precluded a more diligent search on my part.

IRAQ, 2003-4 AND MESOPOTAMIA, 1914-18: A COMPARATIVE ANALYSIS IN ENDS AND MEANS

This paper is a comparative analysis of the linkage between strategic ends with operational ways and means of the current operation in Iraq in 2003-4 and the British campaign in Mesopotamia in 1914-18. The two campaigns took place literally over the same ground. The United States now and Great Britain then both faced significant challenges to project and maintain military power in this part of the world. Moreover, the two great powers inherited daunting civil-military requirements in country. This study has restricted research to unclassified sources on Operation Iraqi Freedom (OIF). Open-source research for an ongoing campaign greatly complicated attainment of a comprehensive understanding of the linkage between ends, ways, and means, but such an option facilitated frank debate with wider dissemination.

The study considers the conduct and integration of both decisive and post-conflict operations. The paper will begin discussion of each campaign with an analysis of strategy. What strategic imperatives necessitated the initiation of military operations in this far-flung corner of the world? What strategic assumptions dictated operational, sometimes tactical, ways and means allocated for execution? How did the strategy change over time, in particular during the course of operational execution of both decisive and post-conflict operations?

Historical analysis often carries the burden to demonstrate clear lessons. This comparative analysis did not set out to prove any specific "lessons learned." Rather, the author believes in the value of history to provide "points of departure" for problem solving and dilemma resolution. The course of research and interpretation of evidence has unearthed significant insights into the British experience then vis-à-vis the American experience now. This paper is too late to affect what has already happened in Iraq in 2003, but it provides insights relevant to the continued American presence in Iraq and for future deployments.

MESOPOTAMIA, 1914-18: SWEEPING SUCCESS, DISASTER, AND RECOVERY

The British campaign in Mesopotamia during the First World War was primarily an Indian Army operation. British rule in India was a very unique element of the age of imperialism. The first section will thus provide an introduction to the British Raj and the old British-Indian Army.

THE BRITISH RAJ: A PRIMER

British India encompassed what today are India, Pakistan, and Bangladesh.[1] British control in India underwent drastic revision following the Indian Mutiny of 1857. In brief, the Mutiny ended the political role of the Honourable East India Company. A select, chosen, British aristocracy governed India and controlled the Indian Civil Service (ICS). They were forbidden to own land in India and to participate in trade. Unlike in Britain, they obtained their jobs through open, competitive examinations.[2]

The British Cabinet in London appointed a Viceroy as senior head. He did not rise from within the ranks of the British-Indian aristocracy. He was even more an outsider in that sense. The Viceroy was answerable to His Majesty's Government (HMG). His supervisory chain went back to the Secretary of State for India at the India Office in England, who was a Cabinet Minister, and hence ultimately answerable to Parliament. Viceroys who operated with excessive independence faced recall.[3] This methodology granted the Viceroy considerable latitude, understandable in an age of limited communications.[4] The Viceroy had a Council of five or six, of whom one third to one half were outsiders in the same sense as he.[5] This Council, a critical component of British rule in India, originally included a Military Member.[6]

The Secretary of State for India also selected a Commander-in-Chief, India (C-in-C, India). The C-in-C, India was separate from the British Army's Chief, Imperial General Staff (CIGS). Field Marshal Lord Kitchener of Khartoum's tenure as C-in-C, India between 1899-1906 marked three milestones. Following the elimination of the three Presidency Armies of Bengal, Bombay, and Madras in 1895, he integrated all regiments within a single scheme of numbering and titles. The second established nine permanent divisions with fixed brigades. The third abolished the Military Member of the Viceroy's Council after a bitter, internecine political struggle with the Viceroy, Lord Curzon. The Viceroy and C-in-C became the most powerful men in India.[7]

Leaders did not expect large-scale Indian Army participation in a world war. Diplomatic reconciliation with Russia in 1906 removed the long-time fear of a Muscovite invasion, but the Amir's turbulent kingdom in Afghanistan and the volatile border tribes provided the Indian Army with missions enough. This North West Frontier and internal order were the principal missions, in accordance with extant constitutional practice, whereby the Army in India's role was limited to defense and the maintenance of internal order.[8] Moreover, the Indian Army was not designed for distant expeditionary operations, especially against a modernized, regular army.

STRATEGY AND CONVENTIONAL OPERATIONS IN MESOPOTAMIA

There was neither intent nor a plan to conduct operations in Mesopotamia upon the outbreak of the First World War. The Government of India and Her Majesty's Government had discussed the participation of the Indian Army in imperial missions beyond South East Asia upon the outbreak of war. India agreed to provide troops to France and Aden.[9] Subsequently, they sent an expeditionary force to East Africa as well.

The region first entered the strategic realm on 25 August 1914 with a requirement for the India Office to prepare a ground force to guard the scattered refineries of the Anglo-Persian Oil Company from Abadan Island and gunboats to secure the Shatt-al-Arab estuary.[10] This mission in modern parlance was a force deterrent option (FDO). The 16th Indian Brigade Group under Brig. Gen. W. S. Delamain reached Bahrain on 23 October 1914. Mesopotamia entered the strategic formula in October with a need for some precautionary action to show British goodwill for the Arabs in the event of war with Turkey.[11] Britain's primary strategic aim was not to protect the oil fields. It was rather to show support for the Gulf sheikhs; to impress the Mesopotamian Arabs, who respected only tangible victory; and to insure that the Arabs did not join the Turks in *jihad*.[12] The British were also concerned with the sympathies of their Indian Muslim troops.[13]

Great Britain declared war on Turkey on 5 November; a contingency operation landed the Brigade at Fao on the sixth and secured the Shatt-al-Arab on the fourteenth. Delamein was under the overall command of Lt. Gen. Sir Arthur Barrett, C-in-C of Indian Expeditionary Force (IEF) D, even though the parent 6th Indian Division would not be complete until mid-December. Nonetheless, the British then decided to go for Basra, thus reinforcing success. Boldness paid off when Basra fell on 22 November. Operations continued north to ensure the port's security, and the British took Qurna on 9 December.

The British decision to exploit further for Baghdad itself lies at the heart of the controversy over British strategy.[14] Both the Viceroy and the C-in-C, India agreed that the force available could not exceed a two-division corps due to other commitments: II Indian Corps under Lt. Gen. John Nixon with the 6th and 12th Indian Divisions.[15] There would be no reinforcements. This buildup to two divisions alone took until April 1915, and the two divisions were still not at 100 percent strength, especially in transport.[16]

IEF D resumed the advance in May 1915. Nixon had replaced Barrett on 9 April. Maj. Gen. Sir Charles Townshend's 6th Indian Division spearheaded the offensive. Their victories in spite of severe environmental conditions, paltry logistical capability, and the hardships of the troops remain wonders today. Amara fell on 3 June; Nasiriya, 25 July; Kut al Amara, 28 September.

The string of British triumphs ceased at Ctesiphon on 21 November, when the Turks repulsed all British attacks. At this point the 6th Indian Division was nearing total collapse. Indeed, Townshend's assessment of their serious state drove the revised plan to withdraw to

Kut-al-Amara, accepting a siege if necessary.[17] Belated reinforcements would aid the 12th Indian Division to rescue the 6th Indian Division and raise the siege. Unfortunately, the Turks stymied every attempt of the relief force, now under the command of Lt. Gen. Sir. P. H. N. Lake, to break through.[18] Townshend's surrender of the half-starved remnants of 6th Indian Division at Kut on 29 April 1916 turned British successes into disaster.[19]

Failure alone should not be the mere determinant of the wisdom of a strategy. Hindsight makes indictment of the British insistence to push to Baghdad in 1915 relatively easy. Such criticism fails to take account of the changing imperatives of strategy over time, especially during wartime. This study would like to emphasize five points. First, British decision- and strategy-making took careful note of operations in other theaters. They were keen to assess second- and third-order effects with Afghanistan, the North-West Frontier, Persia, Arabistan, Arabia, Egypt, Gallipoli, and the Caucasus.[20] Strategists also understood the fickle nature of Arab support, which rallied to the winner and plundered the loser. Second, the Mesopotamian Campaign brought the Indian Army to a state of strategic overextension.[21] It was a secondary theater, a sideshow among several sideshows, in an environment of insufficient troop availability.[22] The Indian Army was balancing the demands of France, Egypt, and East Africa, while simultaneously executing an unprecedented expansion.[23] The exploits of IEF D to date had been truly admirable. Indeed, they lead to the third point. Continued victory bred underestimation of the Turks. Obviously surprised by the British incursion into Mesopotamia, the Turks rebounded, so the British faced a revitalized foe at Ctesiphon.[24]

Fourth, inadequate logistics capability finally broke down. IEF D's combat service support (CSS) assets were inadequate from the start of the campaign. River transportation was a concern from December 1914 and only deteriorated.[25] Continued tactical and operational success never rested upon a firm support structure. The costly repulse at Ctesiphon broke the back of the administrative services. There was an inadequate appreciation how tactical and operational success rested upon an efficient port operation at Basra and a robust transportation system to project military power and sustain it.[26] One effect was a collapse in medical support.[27]

Two aspects of this logistical breakdown warrant further comment. Strategic decision makers and operational commanders and staff maintained a parsimonious, peacetime obsession with "economy," creating "an indisposition to forward or press demands" regardless of need, and too often in an atmosphere of isolation from front-line realities. They did not abandon this obsession with economy after the war started, despite the fact that Parliament had already approved funding of the Indian Army's expenses on all overseas missions conducted on behalf of the Empire.[28] Certain operational commanders and staff also squelched those who tried to demand necessary resources. The Parliamentary Commission convened to investigate the disaster at Kut thus commented sharply on the glaring failure to anticipate and expedite fixes.[29] There was also the administrative confusion of trying to manage forces who fell under two systems, Indian and British.[30] Kitchener's elimination of the Military Member of the Viceroy's Council forced the C-in-C, India and his staff to do both jobs since the administrative structure and system still functioned as if there were two separate offices.[31] The C-in-C, India could not possibly perform both jobs effectively with active operations on three continents and in the midst of its greatest expansion in its history.

Another deficiency which the Parliamentary Commission cited specifically was the unprecedented volume of correspondence among senior officials marked as "private." The Commission viewed this practice with undisguised concern. They concluded that this departure from practice in effect "dispossessed" the staffs from their superiors. The Commission believed that the staffs could have worked solutions for the logistical shortfalls more easily and faster than otherwise happened.[32]

Finally, the decision making process which pushed IEF D into a march upon Baghdad was unlike anything His Majesty's Government and the Government of India had ever anticipated. The balance in relationships discussed above between the Government of India and the India Office had broken down. The responsibility to capture Baghdad rested with Nixon, his political advisor Sir Percy Cox, and the C-in-C, India Sir Beauchamp Duff, with the support of the Viceroy, Lord Hardinge of Penshurst. They instituted a major policy change reflecting their assessment without adequate recourse to the proper degree of consultation with the Secretary of State for India and the India Office in England. This gap in turn resulted in a dearth of complete information among the British Cabinet. The Parliamentary Commission concluded that the Home Government in London lacked an appreciation of the scope of Nixon's instructions from Duff as far back as April-May 1915, which told him to resume the advance. Moreover, pushing to Baghdad constantly appeared in their discussions.[33] There was not necessarily a conspiracy by the Government of India. Events in an atmosphere of tactical and operational exploitation moved quickly. The triangle of communications flow between Mesopotamia, India, and London left ample opportunity for confusion.[34]

Deliberate, painstaking reorganization and build up took place before the British resumed the offensive. The British War Office assumed operational control from February 1916 and all policy and management from July 1916.[35] Lt. Gen. Sir F. S. Maude replaced Lake on 28 August 1916. The British captured Baghdad in March 1917 with seven divisions in two corps plus a robust theater support structure. Indeed, the Indian Army defeated two Turkish corps in six weeks.[36] Even then, the British did not continue the advance north for another eight months, capturing Tikrit in November 1917 and Mosul only in October 1918. Originally starved of troops and materiel, the Indian Army eventually reached a strength of 420,000 in Mesopotamia.[37]

"POST-CONFLICT" OPERATIONS IN MESOPOTAMIA

There was no more of a plan to conduct post-conflict operations than there was an operational plan to achieve victory. British intervention in Mesopotamia created a political vacuum once the Turks withdrew. Moreover, when the Turks departed, they left a wake of urban destruction, ensuring nothing of use and/or value fell into enemy hands. The British then implemented a highly-successful reconstruction operation. Certain aspects survived through the post-war period of mandate until Iraq became independent in 1930.

The Arabs were receptive to British overtures. The large Turkish administrative machinery had existed largely on paper. Recognized authority rested upon the village headman, tribal sheikh, and local *seiyid*.[38] Thus, local and imposed institutions had remained separate and distinct. The British could still not take Arab support for granted. Arab loyalty went to the winner; any loser was a prime subject for plunder. This reality spelled the difference between relative tranquility and a line of communications subject to constant harassment. The Turks did use Arab irregular units, but these generally participated in conventional operations. There was no concerted Turkish effort against British lines of communications. The threat was the Arab interest in booty.[39] The British also had to show the will to remain in the areas they conquered to maintain Arab support. Turkish retribution in a reoccupied area would have been merciless.

Certain aspects of "reconstruction" reflected military necessity. For example, Arthur Lawley, a Red Cross Commissioner, visited Basra and Amarah in early 1916 in response to a request for assistance from the Viceroy. Lawley noted that Basra had an adequate water supply, an effective "anti-fly" crusade, and sound sanitation. The inhabitants had to conform to these regulations and benefited from them.[40] Basra was the primary seaport of debarkation (SPOD) in Mesopotamia, so the British built numerous wharves, warehouses, railroads, etc. Basra was just one example of massive British investment in infrastructure which demonstrated the will to stay over the long haul and the generosity to make permanent improvements.

Basra eventually set the example for the rest of Mesopotamia's major cities, but the expansion of reconstruction operations all over the country was a major resource challenge following the fall of Baghdad. Politicians in London wanted to preserve the "existing administrative machinery" with participation from local representatives, reducing the British

6

presence to an advisory function. This idea was not viable. There was no existing machinery of government, and Arabs did not come forward initially. Besides assurances of no Turkish return, they awaited news of British intentions for the government after the war.[41]

The British progressed well beyond projects of military necessity. Lt. Col. Arthur Wilson, himself a Civil Commissioner, proudly recorded the growth of a civil administration behind and on the flanks of the Army. Its mission was clearly to replace the Turkish administration, "to make good by successive instalments [sic] the promises of liberty, justice, and prosperity so freely made to the Arab inhabitants at the very outset of the campaign."[42] Gertrude Bell, a civil servant who visited Mesopotamia in early 1916 from Egypt, typified this dedication. Her visit to Mesopotamia became permanent. She commented on 8 February 1918, "We are pledged here. It would be an unthinkable crime to abandon those who have loyally served us."[43]

The very first British action upon entering Basra was to establish "public order" in the city. The Turkish police chief and his staff were gone; looters had sacked the city within forty-eight hours of their departure. British and Indian military police were patrolling the streets within hours of the British entry into Basra on 22 November 1914, but they were few in number. Wilson acknowledged the challenges in forming a permanent police force. Initially, officers were Moslem Indians from the Punjab. They successfully established civil peace by April 1915. They extended these urban patrols to Amara a few weeks later, then Naziriya. [44] Upon occupying Baghdad, the British conducted house-to-house searches for weapons and prioritized occupation of road connections and bridges.[45] The British supplemented military police and troops with two forces. Local headmen formed small patrols in the smaller towns. The British recruited an irregular, district police to patrol the hinterlands. Their name roughly came from the Persian for night watchmen. These district police proved highly successful, relieving the Army of the need to provide many road and river patrols.[46]

An important step in the establishment of a viable civil administration was the painstaking collection, organization, and systematization of information. Reassigned to the Political Department, Gertrude Bell played a key role here. She classified tribal data and other details, beginning with information obtained from the Intelligence Department, then adding updates based upon the continued British advance. By February 1917, she could claim that her office had not only organized a mass of data, but all tribal and some other material was available in official circulars. They had compiled an exact accounting of the country as the British found it.[47] The process had taken eleven months.

Perhaps the soundest success story was in the legal system, which demonstrated by daily action the British reputation for fair, impartial justice. A Senior Judicial Officer and barrister, Lt. Col. S. G. Knox, presided with a temporary/provincial Code of Law, using a combination of Indian and Turkish law, from April 1915. After the fall of Baghdad in March 1917, courts conducted business with an "Iraq Occupied Territory Code" in Arabic. These replaced all military courts for cases not involving the safety of the armed forces. Significantly, the British used the sheikhs and religious leaders in the administration of justice, integrating both tribal custom and Islamic law. This system formed the basis for a unitary Iraqi court system.[48]

British civil administration became pervasive. In the summer of 1917 the senior Political Officer became the Civil Commissioner in Baghdad, who had Deputies in the other major cities. Civil administrators remained under military authority.[49] The junior officials were quite young, often captains and majors from the Indian Army.[50] Mr. H. R. C. Dobbs from the Indian Political Department, became the head of a Revenue Department. A separate Customs Department fell under Mr. C. R. Watkins, who came from the Imperial Indian Customs Service. The British also fostered the development of a press with the establishment of *The Basra Times* on 29 November 1914. It was a government paper until commercialization in 1921. Later, *The Baghdad Times* published in English and Arabic, becoming an Arab government press in 1921. A major from the Indian Medical Service began a civil medical system on 30 December 1914, becoming the first Civil Surgeon. The Port Health and Quarantine Services, a civil service which helped the Army, dealt with plague in the winter of 1916 and the spring of 1917, and the 1918 influenza outbreak, which did not hit Mesopotamia as hard as it did Persia and Europe.[51]

A viable currency system became a necessity in the light of developing revenues from taxation and customs duties. The British began by setting up branches of the Imperial Bank of Persia which dealt in rupees, rather than gold as in Arabia. They still faced the challenge of limited acceptance of paper notes, especially in Baghdad. Constant assessment and timely response precluded a currency crisis, and passed a rigorous audit. The British even implemented an interim postage stamp system.[52]

Finally, the British effort at reconstruction in Mesopotamia included a rough, embryonic form of what today would be termed interagency operations and coordination with non-governmental organizations (NGO). Thus, Lawley commented favorably upon the military cooperation he received. Indeed, he commented that Mesopotamia saw a "fresh recognition" by Army authorities of the Red Cross as an integral part of the military medical service.[53] However, in general there remained a tension between the Civil Administration and the Army throughout operations in Mesopotamia. First, running the civil service was a major drain of military manpower. Townshend commented in late 1915 that he asked in vain for the return of his British soldiers to 6th Indian Division who were functioning as policemen, clerks, and sundry augmentees to help run and protect the river transport.[54] The Civil Administration drew heavily on personnel from India: the Indian Army, the Reserve of Officers, Civil Service, Imperial and Provincial Police Forces, as well as those who had been serving in the Sudan, Egypt, and England. The other major tension resulted from differing attitudes on the Arabs. Civil administrators, whether civilian or military, eventually spent years dealing with the General Staff and military departments who remembered only Arab hostility, theft, and rapacity.[55] However, military officials learned that fining was a more effective retaliation and deterrent against Arab marauders than burning and shelling villages.[56]

The British Campaign in Mesopotamia began as a strictly limited operation. Excessive ambition led to disaster, the fall of Kut in April 1916. An advance to Baghdad in 1915 was indeed a failure in matching ends and means – the proverbial bridge too far. Paul K. Davis titled his 1994 book *Ends and Means* very aptly. However, the modern reader perhaps cannot appreciate how the Government of India in particular was sensitive to any threat of jihad. The threat was no chimera.[57] Driving a political and social wedge between the Arabs and Turks was crucial in Delhi's view, and that course of action demanded military success and support for the Arabs. The need for Arab cooperation became an obsession.[58] The prize would be favorable repercussions in Mesopotamia, Persia, Afghanistan, the North West Frontier, and within India itself. This imperative appeared all the more critical in the light of the failed Gallipoli expedition and the periodic delays in the advance to Baghdad. Basra alone did not meet the strategic imperative.[59] Unfortunately, the use of the Indian Army as an imperial strategic reserve had already expended its available manpower. The Indian Army was in too many locations when the Government of India needed more troops to capitalize upon success and achieve a decisive victory. Overwhelming political need drove a strategy without commensurate means.

The end of the First World War was merely a passing event for the Civil Administration. Mesopotamia became a British Mandate by approval of the League of Nations. Much work remained. The religious question was significant.[60] Achieving a lasting political settlement would prove difficult in the wake of regional diplomatic contradictions like the Sykes-Picot Agreement and the Balfour Declaration, as well as the inability to find a viable, successor ruler in Iraq.[61] Nonetheless, the British Mesopotamian Campaign demonstrated the successful, simultaneous conduct of conventional combat and reconstruction operations.

IRAQ, 2003: THE STRATGEY OF PRE-EMPTION

This comparative analysis views the invasion of Iraq in March 2003 as a comprehensive strategy for the Global War on Terrorism (GWOT), the Middle and Near East, and the wider view of foreign policy, since all are inter-related.[62] The clear focus of GWOT is upon radical, Islamic fundamentalism. Operation Enduring Freedom (OEF) in Afghanistan was a retaliatory strike. OIF is very different. It targeted a potential ally of Islamic terrorists like al-Qaeda. Regime change removed a major destabilizing element in the region, in particular for Israel, Kuwait, and Iran. American intervention to help the Iraqi people could demonstrate the viability of a representational form of government in Arab Moslem states. Toppling the Saddam dictatorship and Ba'athist oligarchy sent a clear, if radical, warning to other potential foes, e.g. North Korea, Iran, and Syria.[63] Pre-emption would also eliminate any weapons of mass destruction (WMD) and punish Saddam Hussein for defiance of UN resolutions.[64]

The Osama bin Laden tape of early January 2004 supports this interpretation. He is disappointed that Arab rulers failed miserably to resist American efforts in OEF and OIF, torpedoing any chance of a great Islamic rising. In Iraq American and coalition forces have begun to turn the tide against a poorly-supported insurgency. Worse, he views the "capitulation" of Iran, Libya, and even Syria as a most unsatisfactory, world strategic situation.[65]

THE ROLLING CAMPAIGN START

The American military conducted detailed, systematic, continuous planning prior to the invasion of Iraq. Indeed, the campaign may be the most planned operation since D-Day on 6 June 1944 and Desert Storm in 1991, although plans changed constantly during the final months and weeks.[66] Two aspects of that planning warrant particular examination. The first concerns the implications, tactical and logistical, of the so-called rolling start. The second concerns the nature and degree of pre-war planning for Phase IV, post-conflict operations.

There was considerable controversy about the operational ramifications of the rolling start. The inability to land the 4th Infantry Division (Mechanized) in Turkey to launch the northern front was a major loss of combat power. Commanders demonstrated adequate combat forces were on the ground to execute the decisive operations. However, success does not mean that more combat power was not needed. Indeed, the sheer rapidity of success with so few troops perhaps led to a lack of Iraqi psychological understanding of the depth of their defeat in so short a time. This study is more concerned with the effects on logistics and post-conflict operations.

The most glaring deficiency for the conduct of decisive operations to emerge from the rolling-start nature of the campaign was a failure in logistics. Very generally speaking, bulk fuel, ammunition, food, and water sufficed, albeit to very different degrees; habitual sustainment was an overall challenge. The timely delivery of Class IX repair parts was an especially-glaring failure.[67] Logisticians at all echelons lacked timely knowledge of actual requirements, visibility of where everything was in the pipeline, and an effective transportation network.[68] There was no deliberate, tiered establishment of a logistics architecture of direct support (DS) and general support (GS) units at corps and theater levels. Worse, logistics units had no priority in the deployment sequence.[69] The sheer effort required for the results obtained to make logistics work, and the hand-to-mouth existence which ensued in certain commodities, are not acceptable standards.[70] While Iraq was very different from Afghanistan, the repetition of certain logistics challenges suggests a failure to integrate lessons learned between the operations.[71]

POST-CONFLICT OPERATIONS

There was considerable discussion over the challenges of reconstructing an Iraq without Saddam Hussein well before the war commenced. Writer James Fallows has articulated convincingly that nearly everything that has occurred in Iraq since the fall of Saddam's regime was the subject of prewar discussion and analysis, laid out in detail and in writing for decision makers, beginning in October 2001.[72]

The breadth and depth of pre-war analysis are impressive. One think tank assessed potential human problems following war.[73] An exceptionally-detailed study identified four broad categories for post-conflict reconstruction: security, governance and participation, justice and reconciliation, and social and economic well-being.[74] The U.S. Army War College's Strategic Studies Institute (SSI) study laid out a detailed Mission Matrix for Iraq with a Transition phase beginning during the Decisive Operations phase.[75] Begun in October 2002, four months elapsed before publication in February 2003. Commentators often view the document as a superb analysis of lessons learned in Iraq. Yet the authors' intent was to publish clear guidelines prior to the invasion.[76] The State Department Bureau of Near Eastern Affairs began a comprehensive, classified analysis in March 2002 which became The Future of Iraq Project.[77] It concluded that reconstruction would require a long-term, expensive commitment.[78]

Two observations emerge from an unclassified analysis of U.S. Government, pre-war strategic planning. First, the plan for the post-conflict phase, due to factors of time available and the mental focus on decisive military operations, was inadequate for the sheer scope of the mission which in fact occurred. A "rolling-start" campaign with its emphasis on rapid "decisive action" and "shock and awe" is far divorced from the mindset to plan the minute detail of the establishment of effective bureaucratic administration and the execution of essential public services over the long term. However, of much greater significance were faulty assumptions at strategic level which refused to credit and accept the detailed, pre-war post-conflict planning.[79] Writer Michael Elliott was specific. He contended that Pentagon plans for postwar Iraq rested upon three assumptions – all three of which turned out to be false.[80] A Noontime Lecture (NTL) at the U.S. Army War College echoed the assessment concerning false planning assumptions.[81]

What did all this mean on the ground? In short, the "rolling-start" campaign concept did not understand or rejected the notion that Phase IV operations required more troops than Phase III. Hence, there were no provisions for the deployment of robust follow-on forces to assume a significant security mission, e.g. more combat units and/or a military police brigade with appropriate subordinate elements. Instead, troops intended to participate in decisive operations, whose deployment was delayed, became de-facto security forces upon arrival in country. Many were already too late to prevent the bulk of the looting, but they did little to stop the looting upon arrival.[82] The decision of Paul Bremer, head of the Coalition Provisional Authority (CPA), to disband the Iraqi armed forces exacerbated the difficulties. De-Ba'athification of the Iraqi military did not require total disbandment. Granted, numerous Iraqi forces simply melted away, but internal disintegration does not explain the entire story. Disbandment created a pool of armed, unemployed Iraqis who became part of the problem.[83]

Likewise, the plan should have "packaged" a significant force of combat support (CS) and combat service support (CSS) units to begin the humanitarian and stability and support operations (SASO). Admittedly, finding the correct mix and number of units was a daunting task – and will remain so. But there was no realistic alternative. The lack of international support reduced United Nations participation to a trickle. Moreover, non-governmental organizations (NGOs) did not flee Iraq only in the wake of the latest terror. The NGOs had largely abandoned Iraq as far back as mid-1992.[84] Those few present in 2003 lacked on-the-ground experience.[85] Coalition troops in fact did well in humanitarian operations – in large measure due to preparedness for worst-case scenarios.[86] However, the CFLCC commander lacked the ground forces and the direction to inaugurate other post-conflict operations with a firm hand.

American military capability in the twenty-first century is undoubted. This superiority notwithstanding, OIF, and OEF before it, appear as attempts to wage war "on the cheap." Stated differently, Phase III decisive operations now require fewer troops than Phase IV. However, while the former wins the war, the latter wins the peace.

"LESSONS LEARNED"

A comparison of the First World War British Campaign in Mesopotamia and the current American/coalition operation in Iraq highlights several differences as well as similarities. In the interest of balance, this study will begin with the differences.

First, there is no real comparison between the levels of strategic and operational planning of the two campaigns. The British had no intent to operate in Mesopotamia in August 1914. They eventually formulated and executed a contingency operation a mere three months later in November 1914. The American operation came after meticulous planning, albeit subject to considerable change and with certain, significant, misconceived assumptions.

Second, conventional, military or "decisive" operations proceeded along different lines. The British had to advance in very distinct phases, in particular after the disastrous surrender of Townshend in Kut in April 1916. Two years and four months passed from the initial British landing in the Shatt-al-Arab to their capture of Baghdad. Conversely, the American offensive was a single, sweeping campaign to accomplish regime change with a swift advance to Baghdad and the rapid overrunning of the entire country. The conventional Iraqi defense was feeble compared to expectations; the absence of urban fighting a pleasant surprise. Pres. George Bush declared major combat operations over in six weeks. The shock came later.

Third, the British faced an easier task in the conduct of post-hostilities operations for one distinct reason. Ineffective Turkish rule over the Arabs left viable, local institutions. The British were able to capitalize upon these local Arab institutions, linked with British organization and concepts of justice and the rule of law to establish political and social order. Their major task was simply to demonstrate British intent to remain. The Americans faced a far more daunting task. The Iraqi people were not just venturing into unexplored ground. A quarter century of unprecedented fear and repression has left the Iraqis psychologically paralyzed in every way, and utterly unprepared to do anything in a cooperative manner. Newfound freedom conflicts with fear of the past and the unknown.[87] Expatriate Iraqi population elements frankly misled planners and/or decision makers and bred misconceptions about how to proceed effectively.[88]

Some fascinating similarities emerge from this comparative analysis. First, both campaigns perforce had to conduct post-conflict operations as a result of successful combat operations. Granted, the initial basic strategies appear to exhibit drastic differences in scale. The British originally intended a peripheral operation to protect friendly Arab rulers and develop pro-British sentiment to preclude successful, Arab-Turkish holy war. The American goal of regime change in 2003 was far more ambitious from the start. But both filled a political vacuum.

Second, this study concludes, rather harshly in some minds, that both the Mesopotamian Campaign through 1916 and the Iraqi Campaign in 2003 were logistics failures. Logistics exerted such significant constraints and restraints as to inhibit commanders at the tactical level. Both the British in 1914-15 and the Americans in 2003 took risk given inadequate logistical posture in theater. Interestingly, transportation shortfalls figured prominently in both campaigns: boats for river transport in Mesopotamia, and trucks for ground line haul and air transport in Iraq. Mesopotamia scandalized the British with the utter breakdown of medical services. In Iraq the breakdown lay in selected supply and services, especially in Class IX repair parts, although asset visibility and distribution management in general failed to meet expectations.

Third, combat operations triumphed singularly against the enemy. The Turks in late 1914 - early 1915, and in 1917-18 and the Iraqis in 2003 were simply no match for their opponents. But these triumphs did not end the fighting. Both the British and Americans still faced chronic threats to their lines of communication. This threat differed slightly in scope and origin. The principal British foe was the Arab raider, interested in plunder and preying upon the weak, losing side. As ultimate British success became more evident, this raiding petered out. The Americans faced a more fanatical, ideologically-motivated threat, which crystallized into an insurgency, one which the American and coalition partners appear to be gradually winning as of January 2004.[89] However, both the British in 1914-18 and the Americans in 2003-4 were fortunate that their opponents had no comprehensive plan to target lines of communication. Otherwise, already-stretched supply lines would have faced collapse.

Fourth, neither the British nor the Americans took sufficient note of post-hostilities requirements in planning. Indeed, both governments, in 1917 and 2002-3, expected short periods of transition to Arab self-rule. Both views were extremely optimistic, if not myopic and fanciful. Defeat of the enemy army brought the fall of the state and left a power vacuum. Both campaigns also demonstrated excessively-optimistic expectations of Arab support, both domestically "in country" and internationally in the region.

Fifth, both the British in Mesopotamia and the Americans in Iraq instituted largely ad-hoc post-conflict operations. In both cases they proved to be very effective over time. Initially perceived as too little too late, post-conflict operations worked in Mesopotamia and are working in Iraq at the time of writing. The British in Mesopotamia capitalized upon a wealth of available talent in officials who had decades of experience in India, Egypt, the Sudan, and knowledge of the Persian Gulf region. They were also able to develop procedures in the Basra vilayet first, before moving onto Baghdad. The Americans faced a more difficult mission, and lacked a similar pool of long-experienced personnel. Nonetheless, adaptable soldiers, many with previous experience in the Balkans, exercised initiative and devised suitable methods. The effort still appears more halting and, indeed, amateurish in comparison. The recent British After Action report for Iraq concluded that a great deal of advance planning must occur "a long time ahead of a decision to undertake the military option" of intervention.[90] A significant mitigating factor for Iraq was that sheer secrecy worked against the ability to conduct in-depth, interagency planning,[91] as the British Mesopotamian "private" correspondence had stymied full cooperation.

Sixth, security became the primary post-conflict mission requirement. In both Mesopotamia and Iraq the interval between the defeat of the enemy's armed forces with the collapse of any residue political authority and the occupation of key facilities and nodes by friendly forces was critical. The majority of the looting took place during this period of unmistakable power voids in both conflicts.[92]

Seventh and perhaps most significantly, the armed forces, mainly the army, became the primary tool of action. The Indian Army in 1914-18 and the United States Army and coalition forces in 2003 conducted nation building because there was no one else able to do so.

RECOMMENDATIONS

This comparative analysis suggests a few key recommendations for senior leaders to consider. First, expeditionary operations in the twenty-first century will likely continue to problem areas of the world. American political leadership may determine another regime change necessary. Intervention may be required in a failed state. Whatever the reason, the American armed forces must be prepared to conduct both decisive combat and post-conflict operations in a theater **simultaneously**. Hence, post-conflict operations require the same depth and breadth of joint and combined/coalition planning **before operations commence** as devoted to the conduct of decisive operations, plus the added complexity of integrated and synchronized interagency planning. Moreover, plans for the Middle and Near East should avoid the temptation to overestimate the scope of potential Arab support for any western intervention operation.[93] Such support for Western action, regardless of the justice or necessity, cannot overcome historical suspicion and resentment.

Second, even the best efforts of the United Nations (UN) and the dedication of non-governmental organizations (NGO) and international organizations (IO) will be unable to accomplish much in the early stages. The death of a state, no matter how oppressive or how feeble, will be a traumatic experience. Invariably there will be significant infrastructure challenges, due to destruction, damage, or simple non-existence. The United States Army will remain the primary instrument of post-conflict operations during initial intervention and for an indeterminate period thereafter. Frankly, no one else has the resources to do the job.

Third, the primary post-conflict mission is to establish security. This requirement will almost always necessitate a dual task, the simultaneous conduct of decisive operations with MOOTW law-and-order missions. A political and societal power vacuum marks this sensitive period. The sooner the occupying force establishes presence, the fewer the losses to wanton looting.

Fourth, Army logistics requires significant overhauling in order to sustain the warfighter effectively in the twenty-first century. The vision for the fixes exists; the issue is funding.[94] The "bottom-line" is that the logistics doctrine which won the Cold War and the First Gulf War is not flexible enough for short-notice, expeditionary warfare. Best-business practices which created efficiencies must combine with more effective, responsive support.

Fifth, the experience of expeditionary warfare to the world's problem areas over the last decade has highlighted significant shortfalls in Army force structure. Simultaneous operations in Iraq, Afghanistan, Kosovo, Bosnia, and the Sinai have severely taxed the Active and Reserve Components alike, given the requirements for both initial-entry and follow-on forces. The strains began in 1995 with the onset of Operation Joint Endeavor. The addition of Afghanistan and now Iraq, which equates to a major theater of war (MTW) given the numbers deployed, has nearly broken the system. This dilemma is the result of Army force structure geared to fight a Cold War gone "hot" during which the nation would have time for a very deliberate mobilization. The need now is to respond to generally short-notice, then simultaneous, open-ended, expeditionary and/or imperial-policing operations.

The Total Army requires radical restructuring between Active and Reserve Components. This restructuring is not about saving Army divisions. Rather, it must deal with the entire range of combat, CS, and CSS units, their specific type, and their proportional alignment among Active and Reserve Components to optimize the capability desired both to implement national policy, and in accordance with the deployment guidelines of the Secretary of Defense Memorandum dated 9 July 2003 entitled Rebalancing Forces. The answers must address not only rebalancing the current ratio, but also the potential need to raise new units. For example, the ratio of transportation truck, water purification, maintenance, or general supply units may switch between RC and AC without changing the total number. Other requirements are small, extremely low-density organizations with highly-specialized capabilities which facilitate deployment of the force or conduct significant infrastructure tasks during the early stages of post-conflict operations. The former category includes the array of transportation units related to movement control and other logistics units who execute port support activities (PSA). The latter category includes diverse units like vertical (construction) engineers, facility/utility engineers, engineer fire fighting detachments, and the rarely-mentioned railroad units.

Sixth, there is need for closer, deeper integration between the Departments of State and Defense. Though not preferred, the British experience in Mesopotamia and the American experience in Iraq – and virtually every "small war' in the twentieth century for that matter – demonstrated that the military must remain in charge of initial post-conflict operations, not only to ensure security, but also to conduct a host of non-combat missions for which the Army alone possesses the bulk of the capability. **These missions begin while decisive operations are still ongoing.** Moreover, their duration is uncertain. Finally, the nature of conflict in the twenty-first century has spotlighted the need for a doctrine of interagency operations in a deployed theater.[95] This study also recommends that such doctrine recognize the initial preeminence of the Department of Defense in an operational theater, to include the commencement of reconstruction missions, then highlight guidelines to determine the optimal period to hand over proponency to the State Department. Such a stage would still involve a security mission, etc., but the senior authority would be the American Ambassador, or some other civilian authority.

This study also highlights the utility of history. There is no evidence planners looked at the British experience. They should have. The British experience foreshadowed many problems the Americans would face.

ENDNOTES

[1]For example, the current Afghan-Pakistani border is nothing more than the Durand Line of 1894. It originally demarcated the border between Afghanistan, the Amir's territory, and the fiercely independent tribes of the famed North West Frontier.

[2]Philip Mason, *The Men Who Ruled India* (New York: W. W. Norton & Co., 1985), 207-8. This book is a rework of two earlier volumes, *The Founders* and *The Guardians*, published in 1953 and 1954 respectively. Philip Mason also published under the pseudonym Philip Woodruff.

[3]T. A. Heathcote, *The Indian Army: The Garrison of Imperial India, 1822-1922*, Historic Armies and Navies Series (New York: Hippocrene Books, 1974), 18-19.

[4]The potential for great autonomy has significant relevance with regard to the Mesopotamian Campaign; this paper will return to this topic later.

[5]Mason, *The Men Who Ruled India*, 208.

[6]Historians find periodic reference to the term "Governor-General-in Council" which articulated the legality of the decisions reached by the Government of India. The term can be confusing because the senior British official previous to the Indian Mutiny was the Governor General.

[7]Philip Mason, *A Matter of Honour: An Account of the Indian Army, Its Officers, and Men* (New York: Holt, Rinehart, and Winston, 1974), 397-99. Kitchener insisted that there should be only one senior military man ito to advise the Viceroy.

[8]Brig. Gen. F. J. Moberley, C.B., C.S.I., D.S.O., P.S.C., *History of the Great War Based on Official Documents: The Campaign in Mesopotamia*, 4 vols. (London: HMSO, 1927), 4: 31. Endnotes hereafter refer to this source as *British Official History*. Constitutional practice is more appropriate than constitutional law since a small number of Indian Army units had deployed overseas for the Egyptian Campaign of 1882 and the First Sudan Campaign of 1884-85.

[9]For Indian Army operations on the Western Front, see Lt. Col. J. W. B. Merewether, C.I.E. and Lt. Col. Sir Frederick Smith, Bart., *The Indian Corps in France* (London: John Murray, 1918; reprint ed., Dallington, England: Naval & Military Press, 1996).

[10] Paul K. Davis, *Ends and Means: The British Mesopotamian Campaign and Commission* (London: Associated University Presses), 31.

[11]*British Official History*, 1: 83, 95.

[12]Davis, *Ends and Means*, 50.

[13]*British Official History*, 1: 112. The Indian Army's composition did not reflect Indian society proportionally in the sense that senior officials recruited based upon their concept of the "martial races" whom they deemed made the most suitable soldiers.

[14]The Government of India provided the higher direction at this stage. They were subject to the same procedures discussed above. See page 2.

[15]IEF D became II Indian Corps because I Indian Corps was in France.

[16]There were subtle differences between an Indian division and a British division, though both had twelve battalions in three brigades. Neither had a regimental structure as in continental European divisions. The major difference was that that an Indian division consisted of nine Indian and three British battalions. The Indian battalions had similar organization to the British, but a smaller authorized strength. Division Troops allocations also varied. Indian divisions had to await the availability of British field artillery brigades, since the only Indian artillery was mountain artillery, the famous screw guns. Indian divisions were also almost wholly reliant on pack animals for transport.

[17]Maj. Gen. Charles Vére Ferrers Townshend, *My Campaign*, 2 vols. (New York: James A. McCann Co., 1920), 1:298, 2:7-8; British *Official History*, 2: 134, Davis, *Ends and Means*, 141.

[18]A. J. Barker, *The Bastard War: The Mesopotamian Campaign, 1915-1918* (New York: Dial Press, 1967), 208 has a map with notes which very effectively summarize the challenges of the relief force. Barker's book in the UK was published under the title of *The Neglected War*.

[19]Townshend's conduct as a prisoner of the Turks caused great outrage in England. This debate has often clouded the phenomenal accomplishments of his leadership of 6th Indian Division through the Battle of Ctesiphon. For example, perhaps the most impassioned work remains Russell Braddon, *The Siege* (New York, Viking Press, 1969).

[20]The *British Official History* traces this linkage throughout its four volumes.

[21]Ibid., 2: 2 briefly discusses the general state of Indian military exhaustion.

[22]BEF operations in France in 1914 crippled the small Regular Army; the Territorial Army took a beating in 1915. Kitchener's New Armies would not be ready until mid-1916, bloodily baptized at the Somme on 1 July 1916.

[23]F. W. Perry, *The Commonwealth Armies: Manpower and Organization in Two World Wars* (Manchester, England: Manchester University Press, 1988), 87-92 contains a succinct discussion of the demands upon Indian Army manpower and the expansion effort up to 1916. Perhaps the biggest hurdle in the expansion of the Indian Army was the availability of bi-lingual, British officers. The language of command in the Indian Army was Urdu, not English.

[24]The British now faced a majority of native Turkish troops, rather than the regular Arab units, who came mostly from Syria and Mesopotamia.

[25]*British Official History*, 2: 18; Great Britain, Parliament, Commissions, *Mesopotamia Commission: Report of the Commission Appointed by Act of Parliament to Enquire into the Operations of War in Mesopotamia Together with a Separate Report by Cdr. J. Wedgwood, D.S.O., M.P. and Appendices* (London: His Majesty's Stationery Office, 1917), 18-19, 36, 43-57 passim, 102-3.

[26]Maj. R. Evans, M.C., P.S.C., *A Brief Outline of the Campaign in Mesopotamia* (London: Sifton Praed & Co., 1926), 45, 54-55 contains a succinct overview of this overextension and the linkage between troop strength and the logistic capability to support them.

[27]*Mesopotamian Commission*, 63-95 are thirty-three pages on the collapse of the medical services alone.

[28]Ibid., 74, 103-7.

[29]Barker, *The Bastard War*, 112 cites one specific example which typifies the attitude. See too *Mesopotamian Commission*, 61.

[30]Martin Swayne, *In Mesopotamia* (London: Hodder & Stoughton, 1918), 29.

[31]*Mesopotamian Commission*, 98-99.

[32]Ibid., 102-3.

[33]Ibid., 17-18, 20; *British Official History*, 1: 238-39. Davis, *Ends and Means*, 71 emphasized the India Office's knowledge gap as six weeks behind during this particular time period.

[34]This issue is complex and complicated. The point is the issue's contributory factor. Space precludes a more detailed discussion.

[35]Formal transfer of authority from India to the British War Office did not change the fact that India still provided the bulk of habitual sustainment out of the port of Bombay.

[36]Lt. Col. A. H. Burne, D.S.O., *Mesopotamia: The Last Phase* (London: Gale & Polden, 1936), 55, 113-20.

[37]Ibid., 109.

[38]Gertrude Bell, *The Arab War: Confidential Information for General Headquarters from Gertrude Bell, Being Dispatches Reprinted from the Secret "Arab Bulletin"*, intro. Sir Kinahan Cornwallis, K.C.M.G., C.B.E., D.S.O. (n.p.: Golden Cockerel Press, [1940]), 9-10. The comments appear in the "Arab Bulletin" dated 5 October 1916.

[39]*British Official History*, 1: 163, 271; 2: 47; 3: 3-4, 56, 199.

[40]Hon. Sir Arthur Lawley, G.C.S.I., G.C.I.E., *A Message from Mesopotamia* (London: Hodder & Stoughton, 1917), 2-3, 17, 32-33.

[41]*British Official History*, 3:254; Lt. Col. Sir Arnold T. Wilson, *Loyalties: Mesopotamia, 1914-1917: A Personal and Historical Record* (Oxford, England: Oxford University Press, 1930; reprint ed., New York: Greenwood Press, 1969), 240-41.

[42]Wilson, *Loyalties*, xi-xii.

[43]Gertrude Bell, D.B.E., *The Letters of Gertrude Bell*, 2 vols. (New York: Boni & Liveright, [1927]), 2: 444.

[44]Wilson, *Loyalties*, 12-13, 65.

[45]*British Official History*, 3: 254.

[46]Wilson, *Loyalties*, 65. Wilson's exact statement was optimistic. The British still had to commit troops for security missions, especially cavalry.

[47]Bell, *Letters*, 370, 378, 397-98.

[48]Wilson, *Loyalties*, 67-69, 144. British success made the Turkish system appear even more heinous and foreign to the Arabs.

[49]*British Official History*, 4: 26. The British also appointed Military Governors.

[50]Edmund Candler, *The Long Road to Baghdad*, 2 vols. (Boston: Houghton Mifflin Co., 1919), 1: 277-79. Candler was a war correspondent in theater.

[51]Wilson, *Loyalties*, 69-73, 289. Dobbs was an Indian Civil Service (ICS) veteran who had traveled extensively in Mesopotamia and Persia before the war. He had also served on the Russo-Afghan Boundary Commission.

[52]Ibid., 283-87, 321-22.

[53]Lawley, *A Message from Mesopotamia*, 4, 99.

[54]Townshend, *My Campaign*, 1: 226-27.

[55]Wilson, *Loyalties*, 12, 54.

[56]*British Official History*, 3: 367.

[57] See Peter Hopkirk, *On Secret Service East of Constantinople: The Plot to Bring Down the British Empire* (Oxford, England: Oxford University Press, 1995) on the Germano-Turkish attempt to ignite jihad in India during the First World War. This book was published in the United States with the title *Like Hidden Fire*.

[58]Ibid., 1: 139.

[59]*British Official History*, 2: 1. The British in fact exaggerated the potentially dire consequences. There was surprisingly little effect in the Muslim world after the evacuation of Gallipoli and the fall of Kut. *British Official History*, 2: 309.

[60]Wilson, *Loyalties*, 236.

[61]Faisal, who had spearheaded the Arab revolt on the Arabian Peninsula, became King of Iraq after the war. This marriage of ruler and ruled was an unhappy one.

[62]"Beyond Iraq," *The Stratfor Weekly Online* 21 January 2004 [journal on-line]; available from <http://www.stratfor.com>; Internet; accessed 23 January 2004 appeared after the author wrote this section. It too sees American intervention in Iraq with multiple, strategic purposes; their analysis: to demonstrate the ability to conduct extensive military operations to conclusion, despite casualties, and a geopolitical victory to change several Arab countries' behavior given Iraq's central position in the region.

[63]Tom Friedman, writer and commentator, Television interview by Tim Russert, 20 September 2003. Friedman provided a foundation of sorts to develop these ideas. The author tied together the multiple objectives for war.

[64]The issues of the weapons of mass destruction (WMD) and Saddam Hussein's chronic defiance of United Nations resolutions have become highly politicized, both domestically and internationally. The author believes they are too narrow in scope as a solitary *casus belli*.

[65]"Bin Laden Tape: Honesty and Gloom," *The Stratfor Weekly Online* 7 January 2004 [journal on-line]; available from http://www.stratfor,com>; Internet; Accessed 14 January 2004. The article's assessment sees two likely al Qaeda actions, the assassination of Pres. / Gen. Pervez Musharref of Pakistan and the overthrow of the Saudi regime. The issue of future, direct attacks on the United States remains open, but unlikely in its view.

[66]Strategic and operational planning in the years after the Gulf War of 1990-91, plus the preparations for this particular war, account for the scope and depth of planning.

[67]Several logisticians disagree with this assessment. The ideas in this paragraph are based in part on remarks made by a speaker participating in the Commandment's Lecture Series and "OEF/OIF Logistics Lessons Learned," lecture, Carlisle Barracks, PA, U.S. Army War College, 6 January 2004. This informal discussion among members of the Class of 2004, staff, and faculty crystallized further the writer's estimate. This conclusion remains the author's.

[68]General Accounting Office, *Defense Logistics: Preliminary Observations on the Effectiveness of Logistics Activities during Operation Iraqi Freedom* (Washington, D.C.: U.S. General Accounting Office, December 2003), 2-4, 14-17, 19-22 underlines the problems in asset visibility and theater distribution.

[69]Eric Schmitt, "Army Study of Iraq War Details a 'Morass' of Supply Shortages." The New York Times Online 3 February 2004 [newspaper on-line]; available from http://www.nytimes.com/2004/02/03>; Internet; accessed 9 February 204 and David Wood, "Military Acknowledges Massive Supply Problems in Iraq," Newhouse News Service 22 January 2004 [service on-line]; available from <http://www.newhouse.com>; Internet; accessed 23 January 2004. Schmitt references the Army study by the Combined Arms Center at Fort Leavenworth. Wood cites mostly the Army G-4's assessment.

[70]A recent study cited the primary cause as a lack of "common metrics" between warfighters and logisticians. Gerry J. Gilmore, "Military's Logistics System Found Wanting in Iraq War," American Forces Press Service 21 January 2004 [service on-line]; available from <http://www.afisnews_senderADTIC.MIL>; Internet; accessed 23 January 2004.

[71]These similarities figure prominently in air transport flow, ground transportation, and Class IX repair parts. Generally speaking, the key problems were also asset visibility and theater distribution. General Accounting Office, *Defense Logistics*, 4, 23 cited a failure to incorporate lessons learned from Operations Desert Shield/Desert Storm.

[72]James Fallows, "Blind into Baghdad," *The Atlantic Monthly*, January/February 2004, 54, 56.

[73]Sarah Graham-Brown and Chris Toensing, *Why Another War? A Background on the Iraq Crisis*, (n.p.: Middle East Research & Information Project, 2002), 2, 7, 14. Iraq had an impressive welfare state, which began to unravel in 1990 with the start of the Iraq-Iran War. The study viewed a public health emergency as the most likely, critical challenge and the most frequent cause of death, not hunger, especially for children under age 5.

[74]Ten critical recommendations followed the four broad categories. This particular analysis also recommended preparation for humanitarian support beyond a year. Reinforcing these suggestions were eight clearly-articulated "Lessons Learned" from previous operations, ranging from Haiti to Afghanistan. Frederick Barton and Bathsheba Crocker, *A Wiser Peace: An Action Strategy for a Post-Conflict Iraq*. (n.p.: Center for Strategic and International Studies, 2003), 11-25.

[75]Transition itself consists of four sub-phases: Security, Stability, Build Institutions, and Handover. The matrix lays out no less than 135 tasks for execution: 35 critical, 32 essential, and 62 important ones. Conrad C. Crane and W. Andrew Terrill. *Reconstructing Iraq: Insights, Challenges, and Missions for Military Forces in a Post-Conflict Scenario*, (Carlisle, PA: U.S. Army War College Strategic Studies Institute (SSI), 2003), 44-47. The Matrix itself is on 63-72.

[76]The specific source is currently based on non-attribution.

[77]Fallows, "Blind into Baghdad," 56-58.

[78]George Packer, "Letter from Baghdad: War after War," *The New Yorker*, 24 November 2003, 62. Packer noted that the State Department included sixteen groups of Iraqi exiles.

[79]Fallows, "Blind into Baghdad," 54; Packer, "Letter from Baghdad," 67.

[80]These were that oil would fund reconstruction, Iraqi troops would help keep the peace, and resistance would fade quickly. Indeed, he termed the situation in September 2003 as "Superbowl Jihad." A non-attributable source believes that Elliott was able to talk to several points of contact within the Army to draw these conclusions. Michael Elliott, "3 Flawed Assumptions about Postwar Iraq," *Time*, 22 September 2003, 30-31.

[81]The ideas in this sentence are based on remarks made by a speaker participating in the Commandment's Lecture Series. The speaker cited five: rapid establishment of a new Iraqi government, viability of surviving Iraqi security forces, volume of international assistance available, a rapidly-resuscitated economy, and little degree of Iraqi resentment. These could be due to political bias, which ignored intelligence reports and analysis; strategic priorities required a rapid campaign with a small footprint; and/or simply erroneous assumptions honestly made.

[82]Packer, "Letter from Baghdad," 64.

[83]Fallows, "Blind into Baghdad," 74.

[84]Graham-Brown and Toensing, *Why Another War?*, 7.

[85]"Iraq at Peace," *Peace Watch* 9 (April 2003): 2.

[86]Packer, "Letter from Baghdad," 62.

[87]See Cynthia E. Ayers, "Iraqi Resistance to Freedom: A Frommian Perspective," *Parameters* 33 (Autumn 2003): 68, 78-79; Packer, "Letter from Baghdad," 81-83.

[88]Packer, "Letter from Baghdad," 62.

[89]There is much discussion over the Army need to "rediscover" counter-insurgency techniques. See Conrad C. Crane, *Avoiding Vietnam: The U.S. Army's Response to Defeat in Southeast Asia* (Carlisle, PA: U.S. Army War College Strategic Studies Institute (SSI), 2002). A good perspective at tactical level, which does not deny the ever-present element of uncertainty, is Peter Maas, "Professor Nagl's War," *The New York Times Online* 11 January 2004 [newspaper on-line]; available from http://graphics7.nytimes.com/images/dropcap/u.gif. Internet; accessed 14 January 2004.

[90]Great Britain, Ministry of Defence, *Operations in Iraq: Lessons for the Future*, 69. The format is that of a slide presentation.

[91]Packer, "Letter from Baghdad," 64.

[92]The Iraq portion in this paragraph is based on remarks made by a speaker participating in the Commandment's Lecture Series.

[93]In the case of Mesopotamia, see the frank admission in *British Official History*, 1: 88.

[94]David Wood, "Military Acknowledges Massive Supply Problems in Iraq," Newhouse News Service 22 January 2004 [service on-line]; available from <http://www.newhouse.com>; Internet; accessed 23 January 2004.

[95]In other words, develop a document which would form the doctrinal foundation at interagency level above Joint Publication 3-08, *Interagency Coordination*. William Flavin, "Planning for Conflict Termination and Post-Conflict Success," *Parameters* 33 (Autumn 2003): 95-112 provides a starting point for discussion.

BIBLIOGRAPHY

Mesopotamia

Barker, A. J. The Bastard War: *The Mesopotamian Campaign of 1914-1918*. New York: Dial Press, 1967.

Bell, Gertrude. *The Arab War: Confidential Information for General Headquarters from Gertrude Bell, Being Dispatches Reprinted from the Secret "Arab Bulletin."* With an Introduction by Sir Kenahan Cornwallis, K.C.M.G., C.B.E., D.S.O. N.p.: Golden Cockerel Press, [1940].

_____. *The Letters of Gertrude Bell*. 2 vols. New York: Boni & Liveright, [1927].

Braddon, Russell. *The Siege*. New York: Viking Press, 1970.

Burne, Lt. Col. A. H., D.S.O. *Mesopotamia: The Last Phase*. London: Gale & Polden, 1936.

Candler, Edmund. The Long Road to Baghdad, 2 vols. Boston: Houghton Mifflin Co., 1919.

Davis, Paul K. *Ends and Means: The British Mesopotamian Campaign and Commission*. London: Associated University Presses, 1994.

Egan, Eleanor Franklin. *The War in the Cradle of the World*. New York: Harper & Row, 1918.

Evans, Maj. R. *A Brief Outline of the Campaign in Mesopotamia*. London: Gifton Praed & Co., 1926.

Great Britain. Parliament. Commissions. Mesopotamia Commission: *Report of the Commission Appointed by Act of Parliament to Enquire into the Operations of War in Mesopotamia Together with a Separate Report by Cdr. J. Wedgwood, D.S.O., M.P. and Appendices*. London: His Majesty's Stationery Office, 1917.

Heathcote, T. A. *The Indian Army: the Garrison of British Imperial India, 1822-1922*. Historic Armies and Navies Series. Hippocrene Books, 1974.

Lawley, Hon. Sir Arthur, G.C.S.I., G.C.I.E., *A Message from Mesopotamia*. London: Hodder & Stoughton, 1917.

Mason, Philip. *A Matter of Honour: An Account of the Indian Army, Its Officers, & Men*. New York: Holt, Rinehart, & Winston, 1974.

_____. *The Men Who Ruled India*. New York: W. W. Norton & Co., 1985.

Moberly, Brig. Gen. F. J. *Official History of the Great War. The Campaign in Mesopotamia*, 4 vols. London: His Majesty's Stationery Office, 1923-27.

Perry, F. W. *The Commonwealth Armies: Manpower and Organization in Two World Wars*. Manchester, England: Manchester University Press, 1988.

Swayne, Martin. *In Mesopotamia*. London: Hodder & Stoughton, 1918.

Townshend, Maj. Gen. Charles Vére Ferrers, K.C.B., D.S.C. *My Campaign*. 2 vols. New York: James A. McCann Co., 1927.

Trench, Charles Chenevix. *The Indian Army and the King's Enemies, 1900-1947*. New York: Thames & Hudson, 1988.

Wilson, Lt. Col. Sir Arnold T. *Loyalties: Mesopotamia, 1914-1917: A Personal and Historical Record*. London: Oxford University Press, 1930. Reprint ed., New York: Greenwood Press, 1969.

Iraq, 2003-4

Ayers, Cynthia E. "Iraqi Resistance to Freedom: A Frommian Perspective." *Parameters* 33 (Autumn 2003): 68-84.

Barone, Michael. "Iraq in Historical Perspective." *U.S. News & World Report*, 22 September 2003, 30.

Barton, Frederick and Crocker, Bathsheba. *A Wiser Peace: An Action Strategy for a Post-Conflict Iraq*. N.p.: Center for Strategic and International Studies, 2003.

"Beyond Iraq." *The Stratfor Weekly Online* 21 January 2004. Journal on-line. Available from <http://www.stratfor.com>. Internet. Accessed 23 January 2004.

"Bin Laden Tape: Honesty and Gloom." *The Stratfor Weekly Online* 7 January 2004. Journal on-line. Available from <http://www.stratfor.com>. Internet. Accessed 14 January 2004.

Brooks, David. "Building Democracy Out of What." *Atlantic Monthly*, June 2003, 28-29.

Crane, Conrad. "Lessons of Germany." Interview by Tom Moran. *Newark Star Ledger*, 31 August 2003, 1, 6.

Crane, Conrad and Terrill, W. Andrew. *Reconstructing Iraq: Insights, Challenges, and Missions for Military Forces in a Post-Conflict Scenario*. Carlisle, PA: U.S. Army War College Strategic Studies Institute (SSI), 2003.

Dowd, Alan W. "Thirteen Years: The Causes and Consequences of the War in Iraq." *Parameters* 33 (Autumn 2003): 46-60.

Elliot, Michael. "Facing Reality." *Time*, 22 September 2003, 26-32.

_____. "3 Flawed Assumptions." *Time*, 22 September 2003, 30-33.

Fallows, James. "Blind into Baghdad." *The Atlantic Monthly*, January/February 2004, 52-74.

Fang, Bay. "Help Wanted." *U.S. News & World Report*, 15 September 2003, 14-17.

_____. "In Iraq, Some New Faces." *U.S. News & World Report*, 22 September 2003, 23-24.

_____. "Terror in a Holy Place." *U.S. News & World Report*. 8 September 2003, 20-22.

Flavin, William. "Planning for Conflict Termination and Post-Conflict Success." *Parameters* 33 (Autumn 2003): 95-112.

Friedman, Tom, writer and commentator. Television interview by Tim Russert, 20 September 2003.

Gibbs, Nancy. "After 9/11: Where Do We Go from Here?" *Time*, 15 September 2003, 36-37.

Gilmore, Gerry J. "Military's Logistics System Found Wanting in Iraq War." American Forces Press Service 21 January 2004. Service on-line. Available from <http://www.afisnews_senderADTIC.MIL>. Internet. Accessed 23 January 2004.

Graham-Brown, Sarah and Toensing, Chris. *Why Another War? A Background on the Iraq Crisis*. N.p.: Middle East Research & Information Project, 2002.

Great Britain. Foreign and Commonwealth Office. *Iraq and the UN*. Iraq Briefing Note. February 2003.

Great Britain. Ministry of Defence. *Operations in Iraq: Lessons for the Future*.

"Iraq at Peace." *Peace Watch* 9 (April 2003): 1-2, 9.

"Iraq in Focus." *Peace Watch* 9 (February 2003): 6-7, 11.

"Iraq Moving Forward." *Peace Watch* 9 (June 2003): 6-8.

Lemann, Nicholas. "Comment: Real Reasons." *The New Yorker*, 22 September 2003, 81-82.

Maass, Peter. "Professor Nagl's War." *The New York Times Online* 11 January 2004. Newspaper on-line. Available from <http://graphics7.nytimes.com/images/dropcap/u.gif>. Internet. Accessed 14 January 2004.

Mazzetti, Mark and Whitelaw, Kevin. "Troops or Consequences." *U.S. News & World Report*, 1 September 2003, 16-21.

Mylroie, Laurie. "No Deception on Iraq." *Newark Star Ledger*, 29 June 2003, 1,6.

Packer, George. "Letter from Baghdad: War after War." The New Yorker. 24 November 2003, 58-85.

Ratnesar, Romesh. "Al-Qaeda's New Home." Time. 15 September, 2003, 60-61.

Schadlow, Nadia. "War and the Art of Governance." *Parameters* 33 (Autumn 2003): 85-94.

Schmitt, Eric. "Army Study of Iraq War Details a 'Morass' of Supply Shortages." *The New York Times Online* 3 February 2004. Newspaper on-line. Available from http://www.nytimes.com/2004/02/03>. Internet. Accessed 9 February 204.

Terrill, W. Andrew. *Nationalism, Sectarianism, and the Future of the U.S. Presence in Post-Saddam Iraq*. Carlisle, PA: U.S. Army War College Strategic Studies Institute (SSI), 2003.

U.S. General Accounting Office. *Defense Logistics: Preliminary Observations on the Effectiveness of Logistics Activities during Operation Iraqi Freedom* . Washington, D.C.: U.S. General Accounting Office, December 2003.

Vitagliano, Marissa, et. al. *Reconstructing Iraq: A Guide to the Issues*. N.p., Open Society Institute and the United Nations Freedom Foundation, 2003.

Weisman, Steven R. "Audience Unmoved During Bush's Address at the U.N." *The New York Times Online* September 2003. Newspaper on-line. Available from http://graphics7.nytimes.com/images/dropcap/u.gif. Internet. Accessed 25 September 2003.

Wood, David. "Military Acknowledges Massive Supply Problems in Iraq." Newhouse News Service, 22 January 2004. Service on-line. Available from <http://www.newhouse.com>. Internet. Accessed 23 January 2004.

www.ingramcontent.com/pod-product-compliance
Lightning Source LLC
Chambersburg PA
CBHW061940280526
45787CB00004B/1668